ALL AROUND

God's
Love Letter
Lullaby

Words by Melissa Monroe   Art by Grace a Karidi

The Lord your God is in your midst,
A mighty one who will save;
He will rejoice over you with gladness;
He will quiet you by His love;
He will exult over you with loud singing.

Zephaniah 3:17

God is around
He is all around

He is in the wind
He is not bound

God is in your heart
He is here to be praised

He loves to be loved and
He wants His name raised

He is also near
to protect and to save

Our loving God helps us
to be big & brave

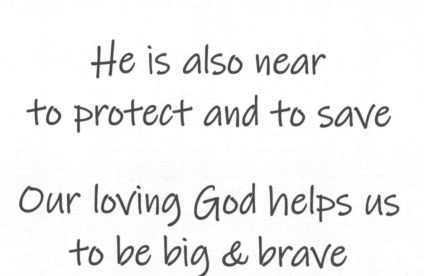

All these things are mysterious and true

Oh God is bigger than me and you

TRUE

He wants you to know
He is mighty and strong

And it pleases Him
when you know you belong

when He thinks of you
His heart expands

He even sings over you and
holds your hand

So, if you ever feel lonely and
you are wondering along the way

Know my dear child as you tarry on
God is never ever far away

Melissa Monroe
is a designer, entrepreneur,
and author from Texas
who now loves to write

Sabeena Karnik
is a paper artist and illustrator
from Mumbai, India
All Around is her debut illustrated book

God's story
is His lullaby to you
It is engraved in stone

WestBow Press books may be ordered through booksellers or by contacting:

WestBow Press
A Division of Thomas Nelson & Zondervan
1663 Liberty Drive
Bloomington, IN 47403
www.westbowpress.com
844-714-3454

Cover & Interior Illustrations Credit: Sabeena Karnik

ISBN: 978-1-6642-9017-4 (sc)
ISBN: 978-1-6642-9019-8 (hc)
ISBN: 978-1-6642-9018-1 (e)

Library of Congress Control Number: 2023901197
Print information available on the last page.
WestBow Press rev. date: 05/18/2023

WestBow
PRESS
A DIVISION OF THOMAS NELSON
& ZONDERVAN

He is ALL AROUND

He is

You are
not alone

Printed in the United States
by Baker & Taylor Publisher Services